Collection : sites and monuments of Tunisia

KAIROUAN

History of the city and its monuments

Text by
Khaled MAOUDOUD
Researcher at the National
Institute of Archaeology and Art
Curator of the Raqqada Museum

National Heritage Agency

National Heritage Agency Press 1992
Design : Abderrazak Khechine NHA Press Services
Colour selection : Grafi - Center
Translated from French by : Anne-Marie Ward-Driss

Within the framework of a vast programme of research and enhancement of the national heritage, the National Heritage Agency has launched a series of publications presenting the principal sites, monuments and museums of Tunisia.

Conceived on the basis of a well researched and richly illustrated text, this collection will no doubt prove a valuable cultural asset in the hands of a large Tunisian and foreign public.

The present book : «Kairouan : history of the city and its monuments» inaugurates the collection.

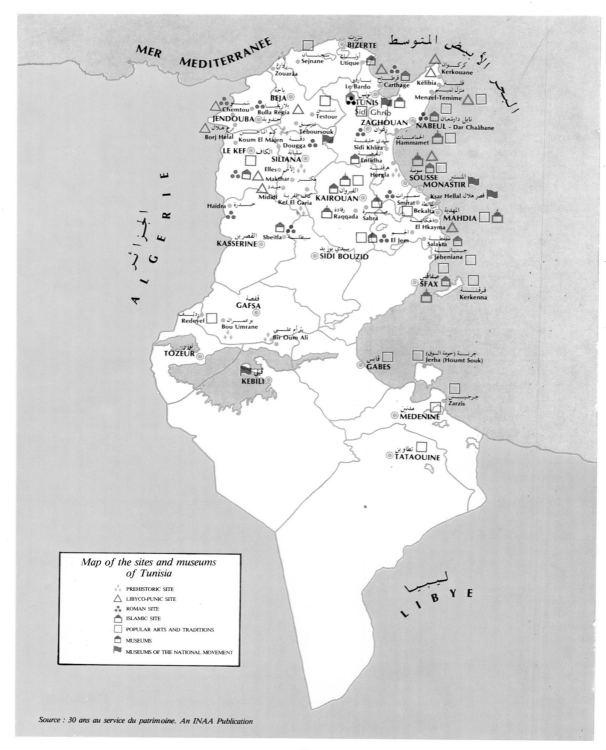

MER MEDITERRANEE

البحر الأبيض المتوسط

ALGERIE
الجزائر

LIBYE
ليبيا

BIZERTE بنزرت
Sejnane سجنان
Zouaâa زوارع
Utique أوتيك
Kerkouane كركوان
Le Bardo باردو
Carthage قرطاج
Kélibia قليبية
Menzel-Temime منزل تميم

BEJA باجة
Chemtou شمتو
Bulla Regia بلاريجيا
Testour تستور
TUNIS تونس
Sidi Ghrib سيدي غريب
ZAGHOUAN زغوان
NABEUL - Dar Chaâbane نابل دارشعبان

JENDOUBA جندوبة
Téboursouk تبرسق
Borj Helal برج هلال
Koum El Majen
Dougga دقة
Sidi Khlifa سيدي خليفة
Hammamet الحمامات

LE KEF الكاف
SILIANA سليانة
Elles الاّلس
Enfidha النفيضة
Hergla هرقلة
SOUSSE سوسة
MONASTIR المنستير

Makthar مكثر
Mididi
Kef El Garia كاف الغارية
KAIROUAN القيروان
Smirat سميرات
Bekalta بقالطة
Ksar Hellal قصر هلال
MAHDIA المهدية

Haidra حيدرة
Raqqada رقادة
Sabra صبرة
El Hkayma
El Jem الجم
Salakta
Jebeniana جبنيانة

Sbeitla سبيطلة
KASSERINE القصرين
SIDI BOUZID سيدي بوزيد
SFAX صفاقس
Kerkenna قرقنة

GAFSA قفصة
Redeyef رديّف
Bou Umrane بوعمران
Bir Oum Ali بئر أم علي
Jerba (Houmt Souk) جربة (حومة السوق)

TOZEUR توزر
KEBILI قبلي
GABES قابس
Zarzis جرجيس

MEDENINE مدنين

TATAOUINE تطاوين

Source : 30 ans au service du patrimoine. An INAA Publication

Map of the sites and museums of Tunisia

- ∴ PREHISTORIC SITE
- △ LIBYCO-PUNIC SITE
- ♣ ROMAN SITE
- ⌂ ISLAMIC SITE
- ☐ POPULAR ARTS AND TRADITIONS
- ⌂ MUSEUMS
- ⚑ MUSEUMS OF THE NATIONAL MOVEMENT

PREFACE

This book is a window open on a great historical city. It does not pretend to present an exhaustive picture of the past, such as can be found in specialized works of greater scope. Its purpose is to awaken the curiosity of the reader. It relates the principal events, from the foundation of a military base to the creation of a city that contributed substantially to the edification of the Arab Maghreb. It was all at once a hive of civilization, the seat of the government and an ideological and political centre. To there men converged to construct a new society that left its stamp on the spirit of mankind.

Through this window we glimpse at the birth of the city, the reasons that led to its foundation, and the various stages of its political existence and we conclude with a visit to its archaeological monuments, and most particularly to Oqba b. Nafi's mosque.

In itself a veritable museum of Islamic arts and civilization, set up by the Association for the safeguard of the city, with its own resources and thanks to the zeal of its members and the support of the National Institute of Archaeology and Arts.

In presenting the city of Kairouan in the light of both its urban and artisitc existence, this work inaugurates a series, the aim of which is to introduce, in a clear and straightforward manner, several cities belonging to the national heritage to visitors eager both to admire architectural beauty and to become acquainted with the culture of other peoples. Thus, this book constitutes a bridge that will lead our visitors to discover the people who built the city of Kairouan and who jealously preserved it so that it might become one of the jewels of our universal heritage.

Mr Khaled Maoudoud has presented us here with a well researched and well presented book. It is, we believe, a reliable and serious, work.

Brahim CHABBOUH
Director of Research
Director General of the National Library

Historical background of the city

THE FOUNDATION OF KAIROUAN

When Oqba. b. Nafi was appointed governor of Ifriqiya and arrived in the year 50 H (AD 670) his primary objective was to establish a stable base for the operations of the Arab army. A position that would enable him to push on with the conquest and at the same time afford him the possibility of retreat within the country in case of threat.

Thus, the foundation of the camp-site (Qayrawan) by Oqba b. Nafi was dictated primarily by strategic considerations. Situated at the centre of the country on a plain half-way between the east coast and the great Dorsale ridge of mountains, al-Qayrawan was set well away from the mountainous homes of the Berber tribes and more than 60 km away from the coast which was still controlled by the Byzantine fleets.

The history of the foundation of Kairouan, the first Moslem city of North Africa, is shrouded in legend and frequently assumes something of a sacred character. Arab chroniclers relate in great, and sometimes fanciful detail, how Oqba, with his illustrious companions, amongst whom several Sahaba, chose the site, and how, after many vicissitudes the city of al-Qayrawan was founded. Oqba proceeded forthwith to the construction of two institutions vital to the city's spiritual and temporal well-being : the Al Jami mosque and Dar al Imara, the governor's palace which together were to constitute the central core of the new city. All around this core, the land was divided amongst the tribes.

From the outset al-Qayrawan was built of stone. The building materials employed were found on the spot and recovered from the numerous vestiges of the antique sites of the region. It was to remain an open city until 144 H (AD 762) at which date the walls were built.

The Arab settlement in Kairouan provoked fierce Berber resistance. For over thirty six years, 50-86 H (AD 670-705) the Arabs faced a succession of incursions from the Berber tribes; the first led by Kysayla who defeated Oqba (killed at Tahuda near Biskra in Algeria in 63 H (AD 683), and then that of al-Kahena, defeated by Hassan b. al-Nu'man, after fierce fighting.

KAIROUAN UNDER A CENTURY OF GOVERNORS

In 86 H (AD 705), under the reign of Musa b. Nusayr, Ifriqiya, which hitherto had been administratively linked to Egypt, conferred upon itself the status of Wilaya and made itself directly dependent on the caliph. Kairouan, which had become a centre of decision, would during the century to come, inaugurate a period of organisation and construction.

The governors appointed by Hisham b. Abd al-Malik were to build fifteen reservoirs on the outskirts of Kairouan to ensure the city's water supply.

Mohammed b. al-Ash'ath, for the first time, in 144 H (AD 762), provided Kairouan with walls to protect if from Berber raids. The walls comprise six gates as well as seven Mahris (guard posts).

Faced with an ever increasing population, the governors appointed by the Umayyad and later the Abbasid caliphs demolished and extended the great mosque three times during the course of this VIIth century.

Yazid b. Hatim al-Muhallabi, 155-170 H (AD 722-728), organised the souks of the city dividing them into specialised areas of activity, as several names of souks reveal : souk al-Ahad (Sunday souk), souk Isma'il, al-Qaysariyya, souk al-Bazzazin (cloth) souk al-Khazzazin (silk), souk al Zaggagin (glassware), souk al-Sayarifa (money changers), souk al-Sarragin (saddlers), etc... Kairouan underwent considerable urban development during this century. The city expanded further and further out. The great mosque and the governor's palace constituted the central core of the city. All the administrative services or Diwan gravitated around this centre : the al-gund (army), al-Kharag (taxation), al-Barid (postal service), Bayt al-Mal (the treasury) etc... It was also from the centre that the principal artery of the city, the simat, and the streets spread out to converge on the squares or Rahba : Rahba of the Qurayshites and of the Ansars. The space was divided into quarters or darb : darb of the Fihrites, of the Banu Hashim, darb al Muhira, darb Umm-Ayyub, etc...

Chroniclers mention the name of several oratoires or small mosques dating from this period : Masgid 'Abd Allah, al-Zaytuna, al-Ansar, masgid Abi-Maysara, al-Hubuli, masgid Abi Sarh...

By the end of the first half of the VIIth century, al-Qayrawan had acquired the infrastructure necessary to its development. It was on the way to becoming the great centre of Moslem civilization that it was.

1 - *Mosque of the Three Doors, an example of the city's many small neighbourhood mosques IIIrd century H. (IXth century AD).*

2 - *Ouled Farhan extra-muros cemetry, XVIIth century AD*

KAIROUAN CAPITAL OF THE AGHLABIDS

3 - The minaret and the two cupolas of the Great Mosque marking the central nave.

The beginning of the Aghlabid rule (AD 800-909) marked a decisive stage in the history of the country. For the first time Ifriqiya, an Umayyad and later an Abbasid province, gained its independence under Ibrahim b. al-Aghlab. Al-Qayrawan, the capital of this dynasty, was to embark upon an era of great prosperity. It was under the Aghlabids that the city completed its process of urbanisation and acquired the equipment and infrastruture worthy of the greatest Islamic cities.

Several outstanding monuments were built by the Emirs of this dynasty :

Ziyadat Allah I rebuilt the great mosque in the year 221 H (AD836).

In 248 H (AD 862) Abu Ibrahim Ahmad extended the prayer hall and built the splendid cupola which surmounts the entrance to the central nave.

In 264 H (AD 860) the same prince gave Kairouan its famous pools considered by chroniclers to be the most important waterworks to have been constructed in the Middle Ages.

Kairouan also acquired several small neighbourhood mosques. Masgid b. Khayrun or the mosque of the Three Doors, 252 H (AD 867) is the most outstanding example. Two royal towns were built in the vicinity of Kairouan :

Al-Abbasiya or al-Qasr al-Qadim, 186 H (AD 801) and Raqqada, 264 H (AD 870).

It was during the course of the IIIrd (IX th) century that Kairouan, on a par with Basra, Kufa or Fustat became one of the most outstanding centres of Arab-Islamic scholarship.

The Imam Suhnun turned al-Qayrawan into a temple of learning and a brillant centre of scholarship and dissemination of Islamic sciences and an important university town.

It was under this dynasty that Sicily was reattached to Ifriqiya.

4 - The Aghlabid pools, IIIrd century H. (IXth century AD)

KAIROUAN DURING
THE FATIMID PERIOD

The arrival of the Fatimids in Ifriqiya in 296H (AD909) signalled a break in the established order. From the outset the new Shiite power was confronted with the grim hostility of the population of Kairouan, long since attached to Sunnism. The Fatimid reign, 296-361 H (AD 910-972) was not favourable to Oqba's city. The Shiite rulers showed no interest in Kairouan, the citadel of Sunnism. They first settled at Raqqada, 296-308 H (AD 916-921) to protect themselves from uprisings and to have an access to the sea.

The third Fatimid caliph, al-Mansur, to celebrate his victory over Abu Yazid «the man on a donkey» built himself a new city two kilometers south east of Kairouan, Sabra al-Mansouriyya to where he transferred all the souks and the industries of Kairouan.

The importance of al-Qayrawan as a centre of commerce declined while Mahdia and especially its neighbour and rival al-Mansouriyya became great centres of trade and administration.

During the first decades of the IVth century H, beginning of the Xth, the city suffered a series of natural calamities : the earthquake of 911, the fire of the souks in 919, floods in 920... From the accounts of geographers and travellers such as al-Yaquibi and b. Hawqal, however, it seems that despite the unfavourable circumstances Kairouan retained its prosperity and continued to drain and to distribute produce from all the other regions.. Its water supply was superior and the Fatimid caliph, al-Muizz «had a pipeline built which, from the mountains would fill the pools, after having passed through his palace at Sabra».

During the Fatimid period, al-Qayrawan was able to maintain and preserve its Aghlabid heritage. This heritage was to flourish during the Zirid period only to disappear with the arrival of the Banu Hilal.

KAIROUAN UNDER THE ZIRIDS

The Fatimid reign in Ifriqiya constituted nothing more than a phase, a prelude to a more glorious destiny, that of reconquering the Caliphate, which according to the Shiite belief was rightfully theirs. The realisation of this oriental dream passed necessarily through Egypt which was conquered in 358 H (969). The Fatimid caliph, al-Muizz, transferred the seat of his caliphate to Cairo in 361 H (AD 972). He entrusted one of his followers, Buluggin b. Ziri, head of the Sanhaga tribe, with the administration of Ifriqiya.

Under the Zirid rule al-Qayrawan was to enjoy relative prosperity but by the year 439 H (AD 1047) which marked a tragic turning point in the history of Oqba's city, it underwent rapid stagnation and a decade later it was destroyed by the Banu Hilal invasion.

Under the reign of the first Zirid sovereigns al-Qayrawan reached the culminating point of its expansion and its population further increased. According to the descriptions of the geographers al-Bakri and al-Muqaddasi, the city was in full epansion. It had 15 main thoroughfares and more than 48 public baths. Its surface had again increased «more than three miles across» specified al-Muqaddasi, i.e. about 5.5. km.

The city's main artery was bordered by a double row of shops and it extended, according to al-Bakri «from Bab Tunis to the north to Bab Abi'l-Rabi to the south, and it measured three miles less a third» i.e. approximately 3 km.

Despite the fact that the Zirid princes resided at al-Mansouriyya, al-Qayrawan thrived on their pomp and the great mosque benefited from their generosity. Al-Mansur gave the building new doors in 374 H (AD 985) and al-Muizz b. Badis had the paintings on the ceiling redone in 414 H (AD 1023) and decorated with a sumptuous ornament of foliated scrolls and fleurons. The same prince endowed the mosque with its famous maksoura.

The Raqqada museum holds a large part of

5 - Painted wood from the old ceiling of the Great Mosque

13

the very rich and beautiful parchment Korans bequeathed by the dynasty to the great mosque as well as the chandelier that lights up the prayer hall and most especially, the famous al-Muizz lantern.

The Kairouan cemetries have also preserved for us some very beautiful funerary stelae from the Zirid era. These stelae are distinguished by their remarkable aesthetic quality and their great ornamental and paleographical richness.

6 - Marble tombstone from Kairouan. Kufic script sculpted in relief. Zirid period, Vth century H. (XIth century AD)

THE HILALI INVASION AND THE FALL OF KAIROUAN

The first Zirid emirs governed the province of Ifriqiya on behalf of the Fatimids of whom they were the faithful vassals. However, by the end of the first half of the XIth century (439H, AD 1047), the fourth Zirid sovereign, al-Muizz b. Badis, had withdrawn his allegiance from the Fatimid caliph in Cairo and recognized the sovereignty of the Abbasid caliph of Baghdad.

In revenge, the Fatimid caliph left Ifriqiya at the mercy of the Hilali tribes. Faced with the imminent danger, al-Muizz called up an army and had ramparts built around al-Qayrawan to protect it, 444 H (AD 1052-1053). His army was however defeated at the battle of Haydaran and al-Muizz was forced to take refuge in Mahdiya while al-Qayrawan was sacked and destroyed in 449 H (AD1057).

The middle of the 5th century H (XIth century AD) marked a turning point in the history

not only of al-Qayrawan but of all Ifriqiya. The breakdown of central power led to anarchy and to the emergence of a multitude of independent principalities.

Al-Qayrawan was in ruins and emptied of its population; its surface area diminished and for more than a century it was to remain in oblivion.

Nonetheless, Oqba b. Nafi's wish to found «a city that would perpetuate the glory of Islam to the end of time» was fulfilled and the religious and cultural prestige of al-Qayrawan was also no doubt the cause of its survial.

With the beginning of the Hafsid period, VIIth century H (XIIIth century AD), the city began to rise slowly from its ruins but it was only in the XVIIIth century, under the benevolent rule of the Husaynid dynasty, that al-Qayrawan was fully restored and again occupied an honourable place within the country.

14

KAIROUAN TODAY

Kairouan today is the seat of a governorate and its population is of over 110.000 inhabitants. Present day Kairouan is composed of the medina enclosed within its walls and of the modern quarters where the administrative services : seat of the governorate, town hall, banks, hotels, commercial centres etc.. are to be found.

The medina of Kairouan in itself constitutes a living musuem of Arab-Islamic art and architecture; its monuments, its souks, its dwellings and its winding streets still bear eloquent witness to its prestigious past.

Kairouan has also retained to some extent its vocation of holy city and it is still the spiritual capital of the country. Religious holidays have a special charm and are celebrated with great display.

The evenings of the month of Ramadhan (month of fasting) are memorable. Each year the city hosts the official ceremony of the Mouled (Prophet's birthday) which takes place in the great mosque and at the mausoleum of Sidi Saheb, companion of the Prophet. Crowds of visitors, both Tunisian and foreign, converge on the city for the occasion.

7 - Kairouan medina, weavers' quarter.

8 - Alley in the medina, evidence of a prestigious past.

9 - The Kairouan carpet, famous throughout the world, is the most highly developped craft of the region.

Kairouan also stands for tradition and this tradition has helped to keep the arts and crafts sector flourishing. The many souks of the city are specialized in various branches of activity; the wool souk, weavers, leatherwork, carvers, the carpet souk where carpets are still sold at auction. These souks occupy the centre of the medina but other activities considered to be not so clean have been relegated outside the city walls, notably, coppersmiths, tinsmiths and dyers. Without a doubt, however, the most highly developed craft is that of carpet making and its work force is made up essentially of women. Kairouan carpets are famous all over the world. The town has however also developed other well known crafts. For example, traditional costume such as the jebba, the pure wool burnous, the hayek (ladies veil), face cloths, saddles, etc...

Finally, Kairouan also stands for an ancestral culinary art : the Makroudh, different varieties of bread, honey doughnuts, lamb couscous are only a few examples of the wealth of Kairouan cooking.

The monuments of the city

1 - The great mosque

2 - The Abou Zam'a Al Balawi mausoleum

3 - The Sidi Abid mausoleum

4 - The Sidi Amor Abada mausoleum

5 - Bir Ruta

6 - The Aghlabid pools

7 - The mosque of the three doors

intra-muros medina

the ramparts

touristic circuit

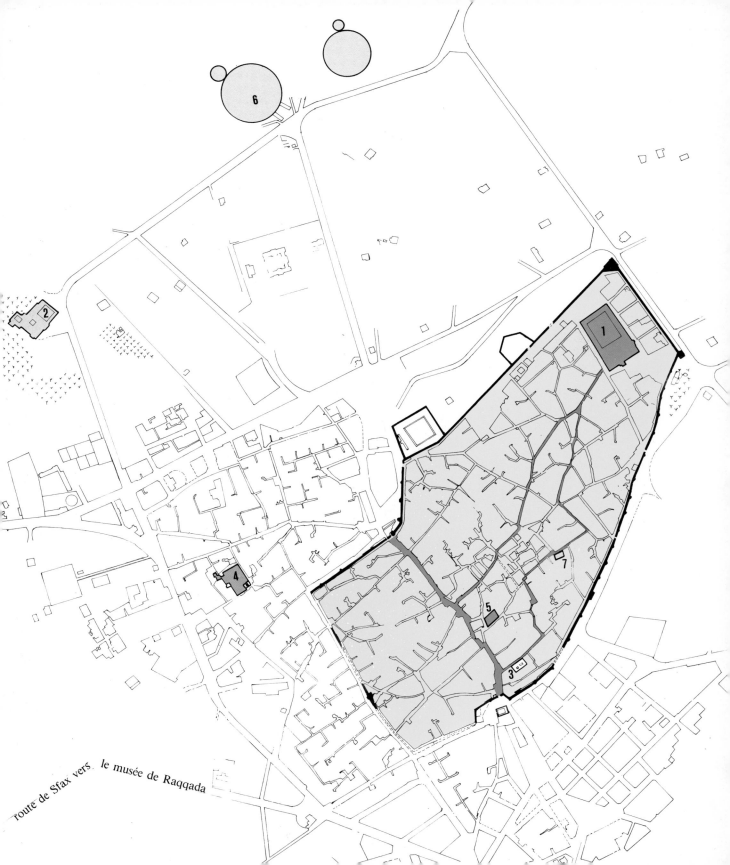

route de Sfax vers le musée de Raqqada

THE GREAT MOSQUE

10 - General view of the Great Mosque.

Once Oqba b. Nafi had decided to transform his camp into a city, he immediately set about providing Kairouan with two fundamental institutions, vital to its spiritual and to its temporal existence : the al-Gami mosque and the seat of the government, dar al Imara.

The great mosque of Kairouan is considered to be the oldest and most prestigious religious building of the western Islamic world. It is one of the rare Islamic religious buildings to have preserved its original aspect such as it was in the first centuries of the Hegira.

Because of the diversity of its architectural forms, the richness of its repertory of ornamental motifs, its Mihrab, its Minbar, its Maqsura, the great mosque in itself is regarded as an important museum of Islamic art and architecture. It also contains one of the richest collections of ancient columns and capitals in the world.

It was Oqba b. Nafi, founder of al-Qayrawan who built the first small mosque out of raw bricks in the year AD 670. It is said that a divine revelation showed him the spot where the Mihrab was to be erected, indicating the qibla, the direction of Mecca. However, the monument we admire today was not built in one go. Each governorship, each dynasty sought to leave the mark of its reign by embellishing, extending or renovating the building.

BRIEF HISTORICAL BACKGROUND

Faced with an ever increasing number of faithful, the governors appointed to rule Ifriqiya by the Umayyad and Abbasid caliphs, tore down and rebuilt the great mosque three times during the course of the VIIth century. Hassan b. al-Nu'man in AD703, Bishr b. Safwan in AD724-728 and Yazid b. Hatim in the year AD 774.

Under the Aghlabids, who ruled over the country during the whole of the IXth century, Ifriqiya unquestionably experienced a period of renaissance. Kairouan developed and was embellished. The Aghlabid emirs built princely palaces in the surroundings such as al-Qasr al-Qadim or al-Abbasiya and Raqqada. They were to undertake three campaigns of work to the great mosque.

The most important of these was conducted by Ziyadat Allah, to whom the reconstruction of the building and the prayer hall are attributed in AD 836. The configuration the mosque

11 - Interior view of the prayer hall.

21

has retained to this day dates from this period. The renovation or embellishment it was thereafter to undergo did not modify its general aspect.

Under the Zirids, at the end of the first half of the XIth century, al-Muizz b. Badis transformed the old Aghlabid maqsura into a library and endowed the prayer hall with a splendid new maqsura.

The Zirids also undertook extensive renovation work on the ceilings.

Under the Hafsids in the XIIIth to XVth centuries, inscriptions still to be found in-situ confirm that these sovereigns undertook important restoration work on a part of the wooden ceiling as well as the renovation of the Lalla Rayhana gate and the construction of its porch.

After the Turkish conquest, the Muradite beys in the XVIIth century and the Husaynids in the XVIIIth and XIXth centuries again redid part of the ceilings, restored the surrounding walls of the mosque and gave the prayer hall new doors.

Today, visitors can contemplate the great mosque with all its history, but despite considerable renovation, it has jealously retained the general aspect it had in the IXth century.

SURROUNDING WALLS, BUTTRESSES, GATES

The great mosque covers a large surface shaped like an isosceles trapezium, its larger and smaller base measuring 74 and 70 meters respectively and its sides 125 and 124 meters. It is surrounded by buttressed walls; the buttresses are set close together and are of varying width, depth and form.

In addition to the buttresses, a glacis surrounds the walls at their base to consolidate them further.

12 - Walls and butresses of the Great Mosque

There are eight entrances to the mosque, six of which give into the courtyard. A door to the east, Bab Lalla Rayhana and the eighth door on the west, Bab al-Gharbi give directly into the prayer hall. On the south end of the building another door leads to the Imam's room and to the library and communicates with the prayer hall through the entrance to the maqsura. The porches with their cupolas surmounting these doors date from the XIIIth century.

13 - Gate : Bab Lalla Rayhana. XIIIth century AD

THE COURTYARD AND THE MINARET

The courtyard occupies the centre of the building and stretches before the prayer hall and its narthex. It had previously been tiled with terracotta tiles but today it is paved with marble.

The surface slopes to force rainwater to run into a small square drain, the ingenious labyrinthic shape of which was designed to decant and filter rainwater.

The dirt is retained on the surface while the filtered water flows into a first decantation cistern and then into other cisterns where it is stored. Several wells with their curbs made from the bases of ancient columns allow the faithful to draw water, in particular for ablutions.

A sun-dial to the east of the courtyard enabled the time of the five daily prayers to be determined, using a clever system of complicated calculations.

14 - Sun dial clock to determine the time of the five daily prayers.

23

15 - General view of the courtyard and the minaret.

16 - Colonnade bordering the courtyard of the mosque.

The courtyard is flanked by two double galleries of colonnades. Several rooms give onto the galleries. The two rooms on the western corner were the ancient Midha (ablutions room). The rooms at the northern end of the courtyard beyond the minaret were the mosques' storerooms where matting, cleaning equipment, oil for the oratory ceiling light, etc were stored. These rooms also stored precious pieces or objects belonging to the mosque and replaced during the course of various renovations and restorations; painted wooden beams dating from the IXth and XIth centuries, chandeliers and very old wooden furniture.

The minaret, wrongly attributed to the Umayyad caliph Hisham b. Abd al-Malik in the VIIth century, is probably in fact the work of Bishr b. Safwan, AD 721—728. In its form and general aspect it resembles minarets of Umayyad Syria. Ancient blocks of stone were recovered and employed to build the base while the upper stories are built with neat layers of carefully hewn quarry stones.

17 - *Minaret of the Great Mosque; used to call for prayer but also as a lookout tower.*

18 - *Minaret door : ancient friezes were used for the jambs and lintle.*

The minaret is composed of three stories of unequal width and height : 10.50 meters wide at the base and 31.5 meters high. Access to the minaret is on the south side, through a door opposite the prayer hall. The jambs and lintle of the door are made from beautiful reconverted fragments of ancient friezes and soffits.

Inside the minaret, a 129 step stair, turning around a central pillar, leads to the top of the structure which is crowned by a cupola set on a squinch. A series of looplights allow air and light to enter.

The minaret is of a monumental character and is outstanding for the elegance of its architecture. Its construction obeyed both religious and military considerations. It was primarily conceived to call for prayer but was also used as a look-out tower dominating the surrounding countryside.

Despite the numerous renovations undertaken during the Hafsid period in the XIIIth and XVth centuries, the minaret has conserved its Aghlabid structure and aspect dating from the IIIrd century of the Hegira or the IXth century AD.

THE PRAYER HALL

19 - Central aisle of the prayer hall.

The prayer hall lies on the south side of the courtyard. It is a pillared room built by Ziyadat Allah in AD836 and extended by his successors Abu Ibrahim Ahmed in AD862 and Ibrahim b. Ahmed in AD875.

The room is 37 meters deep and 70 meters wide. A 6 meter wide aisle runs along the wall of the Qibla and joins the central axial aisle which is 5.75 meters wide, to form a T shape.

26

20 - One of the interior doors leading to the prayer hall.

The central aisle is flanked on each side by eight secondary aisles perpendicular to the transverse aisle. From the transverse nave to the colonnaded narthex, there are seven bays.

The central and the secondary naves are supported by arcades of semicircular arches supported by a large variety of reconverted ancient columns. A springer, an impost and a cornice are interposed between the capitals, and the downward curb of the arches.

The first cupola rises above the mihrab and marks the crossing of the central and the transverse naves. A second cupola surmounts the entrance to the central aisle and constitutes the central motif of the facade and of the colonnades framing the courtyard. The cupolas are set on shell-shaped squinches.

21 - Mihrab cupola on a squinch.

THE MIHRAB

The facade of the mihrab of the great mosque of Kairouan is considered to be one of the most harmonious compositions of Islamic art. This IXth century mihrab, has the form of a semi-circular niche, the superior part of which is crowned by a semi-cupola. It is covered by twenty-eight pannels of marble set in seven vertical rows of four pieces. These pannels are decorated with open work and champlevé and offer a large variety of floral and geometric motifs.

Half way up these pannels, an epigraphic band composed of a line of kufic calligraphy sculpted in relief runs across the width of the niche. The text of the inscription is a profession of faith KOR CXII 1-4, followed by the Taslia.

A wooden semi-cupola crowns the niche of the mihrab. It is formed of curved timber boards covered with a plaster coating and entirely painted : A double foliated scroll unfurles in regular involutions to end in five-lobed leaves, while pointed clusters of grapes and tendrils fill the concavities of these involutions. This elegant ornament is evidence of the skill of the painter and his ability to harmonize colours and oranmental motifs to form his arabesque.

The frame of the mihrab's niche is ornamented with a very beautiful and rare collection of ceramic tiles with metallic glints dating from the IXth century AD. These tiles are both monochrome and polychrome and were imported from Mesopotamia. Each tile presents a different design with subtle combinations of floral and geometric motifs.

22 - Facade of the Mihrab.

23 - Faience tiles with metallic glints framing the mihrab IIIrd century H (IXth century AD).

THE MINBAR

The minbar is situated on the right of the mihrab, against the wall of the qibla. This pulpit is used by the Imam at the hour of the preach.

This jewel of Ifriqiyan art dates from the IXth century AD. It is the oldest dated pulpit of the Islamic world. Built of teak, the minbar is composed of more than 300 sculpted and assembled pieces; the pannels of the pulpit are of an exceptional ornamental richness and illustrate the extreme variety of the repertoire from which the Ifriqiyan ornamentalist drew his models.

24 - Detail of the different ornamental motifs decorating the pannels of the mihrab.

25 - The Minbar; it is one of the most splendid and most ancient pulpits of the Moslem world.

THE MAQSURA

The maqsura is slightly to the right of the minbar and is the work of a Zirid ruler, al-Muizz b. Badis, Vth century of the Hegira or XIth century AD. It is a private enclosure, reserved for the prince and certain members of his court, enabling them to pray secluded from the other worshippers. The maqsura communicates with the outside by a door built in the qibla wall: it is known as Bab al-Imam, formely Bab al-Sultan, and it opens onto the prayer hall through double doors. The epigraphic band in this maqsura is one of the superb examples of epigraphic bands in Islamic art. It uses elegant flowers and braided kufic script sculpted on a background of intertwined plants.

Through its wealth of architectural forms and the diversity of its ornamental repertoire, the great mosque of Kairouan greatly contributed to the elaboration of Islamic art.

The Kairouan school has inspired and served as a model to all the buildings of the western basin of the Islamic world. The great mosque has also played a fundamental role in Ifriqiyan intellectual life. It was one of the foremost centres of Arab-Islamic culture and a centre of scholarship and dissemination of Islamic sciences.

26 - The Emir Al-Mu'izz b. Badis' Maqsura, a masterpiece of wood carving Vth century H (XIth century AD).

THE ABU ZAM'A AL-BALAWI MAUSOLEUM

This mausoleum contains the tomb of an illustrious man, Abu zam'a Ubayd b. al-Arquam al Balawi, one of the companions of the prophet Mohammed.

Abu Zama participated in the first Moslem military expeditions in Ifriqiya. He was killed in the year 34 H (AD654) on one of these expeditions to Djeloula, about thirty kilometers from Kairouan. He was buried on the site of Kairouan before the foundation of the city.

The companion of the prophet is the object of great veneration. Oral tradition holds that he kept three hairs of the prophet's beard and that according to his wish, he is buried with these saintly relics.

The buildings form a pleasing architectural complex composed of three ensembles :
The mausoleum housing the tomb, the cupola and the courtyard.

They are the work of the Muradite Bey, Hammouda Pacha AD1665. The annexes containing guest rooms and the master of the cult's lodgings.

The minaret and the medersa, which includes the oratory, the ablutions room and the studens' rooms.

The latter two parts are the work of Mohammed b. Murad, and were built from AD 1685 to 1690.

27 - The cupola of the mausoleum housing the tomb of Abu Zam'a, companion of the prophet.

28 - *Entrance to the tomb where the master of the cult makes sure that the premises are treated with proper respect.*

29 - *Exterior view of the two cupolas.*

30 - *Colonnades preceding the room with the cupola and leading to the central courtyard and to the mausoleum.*

Access to the three building is through a large square courtyard bordered on three sides by colonnades.

On the left of the courtyard is the entrance to the medersa. The hall turns into a small courtyard framed by colonnades. The oratory is to be found at the end of the north east side and it is used as a prayer hall as well as a classroom. The north west and south east sides are lined with rooms reserved for students.

The mausoleum and the courtyard are the parts reserved for worship of the saint. This is the focal point of the building and the most ornate part of the architectural complex.

31 - Ceramic tiles decorating the walls of the courtyard.

32 - Painted ceiling of the gallery.

33 - Central courtyard of the mausoleum where the official feast of the Mouled is celebrated each year.

The architectural forms employed in the building had already been seen in Kairouan. However, these were combined with a new type of decoration which constituted a departure from the ornamental repertory of the first five centuries of the hegira.

A new conception resulting from new influences led to the use of different forms and decorative styles.

Tunisia was subjected to the traditions, tastes and influences of its new masters : the Ottomans. The exodus to Tunisia of the major part of the Moslems expelled from Spain since the XVIth century added further to the influx of new influences.

Hence, the lower part of the walls of this building is tiled with faience tiles or decorated with polychrome faience pannels. The upper part of the walls are coverd with pannels of exquisitely sculptured or carved stucco displaying an infinite variety of ornamental motifs. The painted wooden ceilings present a splendid foliated design with the stems and the ramifications terminating in a variation of motifs that are an admirable blend of local decorative forms and Anatolian flora.

This architectural complex has played, and continues to play, a socio-cultural role of prime importance. It is Tunisia's most frequently visited mausoleum with visitors coming from all over North Africa to make vows or celebrate weddings or circumcisions. The official celebration of the Mouled, commemorating the birth of the Prophet, is held there each year.

34 - Minaret bordering the medersa decorated with ceramic tiles.

35 - 36 Tiled pannels covering the walls of the courtyard and the mausoleum.

36

THE AGHLABID POOLS

Due to its geographic position and its climate, Kairouan has always fought a relentless battle against drought and supplying the city with water has been a constant worry.

From the early days of Moslem rule in Ifriqiya, the major concern of the governors was to keep the city supplied in water. It is mentioned in writings that the Umayyad caliph Hisham b. Abd al-Malik ordered his governor in Ifriqiya, b. al-Habhab (AD734-741), to build 15 reservoirs on the outskirts of the city to provide the ever increasing population of Kairouan with water.

The Aghlabids (IIIrd century H or IXth century AD) improved and added new waterworks. In 248 H or AD862, Abu Ibrahim Ahmad completed the most famous of these installations : the Kairouan Pools. In their descriptions of the town and its monuments, Arab geographers convey their awe before the majesty of these waterworks, considered to be the grandest ever built in the Middle Ages.

Unfortunately, most of these installations have disappeared and collective memory has retained only the memory of Abu Ibrahim Ahmad's two pools.

37 - General view of the Aghlabid pools : small decantation pool and the larger pool, IIIrd century H. (IXth century AD).

The works are composed of three main elements covering an area of 11,000 m² and with a capacity of 53,000 m³ of water.

The larger pool is round in shape and has a diameter of 127.7 meters and is 4.8 meters deep. An octagonal tower crowned with a cupola stands in the middle of the pool. According to the geographer al-Bakri, this was where the Emir came to rest.

The large pool is supported on the inside by 65 rounded buttresses and by 118 buttresses on the outside.

The smaller pool which is set against the larger pool has a diameter of 34 meters and is consolidated by 17 interior buttresses and 26 on the outside. It communicates with the larger pool through a semicircular overflow. Both pools are built of stone rendered over and rounded at the top.

38 - Partial view of the larger pool.

39 - Point where the two pools join.

The cisterns communicate with the large pool and have a barrel vaulted ceiling supported by arches resting on pillars.

Until the beginning of the century it was commonly assumed that in addition to rainwater and the catchment of sources or underground water, the pools were supplied in water by an aqueduct leading from the sources of Cherichera, 40 km to the west of Kairouan.

40 - Arched opening , an «over-flow» providing for communication between the two pools.

However, recent studies and excavations have demonstrated that the pools' principal source of water supply came from the catchment of trickling water from the tributaries of the Marguellil river.

The small pool was connected by means of extensive pipelines and small dams to the tributaries of the Marguellil river. When the river was high, water was drained by these installations and reached the small pool through an opening; there it was filtered and decanted and when it reached a certain level, it flowed into the larger pool through the overflow connecting them.

The Aghlabid pools impress with their rugged majesty and sober splendour. They surprise with the mastery of hydraulic techniques they reveal and they fascinante with the elegance of their style and harmony of architectural forms.

39

THE RAMPARTS

For more than a century and a half, al-Qayrawan had no ramparts. From its foundation the city was constantly threatened by turbulent Berber tribes resisting Arab and Moslem penetration in Ifriqiya. This Berber threat almost led to the fall of al-Qayrawan on several occasions and it was forced to engage in a permanent struggle to ensure its survival.

Very shortly after its foundation the city was occupied. For five years, the Berber chief Kusayla, victor of Oqba b. Nafi, made Kairouan the capital of his kingdom, from AD684 to 689.

The first Arab defeat was to encourage and stimulate the ardour of Berber resistance and they multiplied their raids on Kairouan.

La Kahena's insurrection lasted from AD695 to 700. In 758 the Warfajuma Kharigites took al-Qayrawan and massacred a part of the Arab population, and notably the Qurayshite aristocracy.

Faced with this perpetual danger, the Abbasid caliph of Baghdad, al-Mansur ordered his governor Mohammed b. al-Ashath to fortify the city. For the first time al-Qayrawan was provided with walls built of clay in 144-146 H (AD762-763). There were six gates to the walls; Bab Abu'l Rabi to the south, Bab Tunis to the north, Bab Abdallah and Bab Nafi to the east and Bab Asram and Bab Salam to the west.

The city also acquired seven Mahris (guard posts). But these fortifications proved insufficient. The walls of Kairouan were destroyed and rebuilt more than seven times.

41 - Partial view of the XVIIth century AD ramparts.

It was only in 1756 that the Husaynite sovereigns again rebuilt the city ramparts. Reconstruction work lasted from 1750 to 1772.

These are the ramparts we see today. They are crenelated, built of solid brick and flanked with semi circular towers and bastions.

The ramparts extend for more than 3,8 km and are from 4 to 8 meters high and 2.70 meters wide. The wall-walk is 1,50 meters wide. There are several gates, notably Bab Tunis, Bab al-Jalladin, Bab al-Jadid and Bab al-Khukha. They all date from 1772.

42 - Gates and bastions of the walls.

43 - Martyrs Gate or Bab Al Jalladin : 1772.

44 - Bab Al Jadid 1772.

45 - Bab Al Khukha 1772.

SIDI ABID AL GHARIANI

46 - Painted wooden ceiling of the Sidi 'Amor mausoleum.

Situated to the north east of Bab al-Jalladin, the Zawiya of Sidi Abid was built in the VIIth century H or XIVth century AD. Its founder, Sayh Abu 'Abd Allah Muhammad b. 'Abd Allah b. Abd al-Aziz al Sba'i, known as Aljedidi, died in 1386. He left one of his disciples as successor, Abu Samir Abid who came from Djebel Gharian and who carried on the task of teaching until his death in 1402. He was buried in this Zawiya which bears his name.

The monument is comprised of three buildings.

— The mausoleum containing Sidi Abid's tomb. It is the most important and the most beautiful part of the monument. Its walls are covered with ceramic tiles and pannels of sculptured stucco. The beautiful painted wooden ceiling is formed by rows of superposed corbels.

— The oratory and the courtyard : A vestibule leads to the courtyard, paved with marble decorated with geometric interlacing. The courtyard is surrounded by a double storeyed gallery. On the south-east side lies the prayer hall with three transverse ailes.

— The Medersa, with the ablutions room (midha) and the students rooms form the third part of the Zawiya.

Several pieces of XIth century decor, the ringed pillars, the capitals and the kufic inscriptions no doubt originally came from the Fatimid site of Sabra al-Mansouriyya and were used in the construction of this building. The Zawiya also contains several tombs, notably that of the Hafsid ruler Moulay Hassan.

Over the last decade the Sidi Abid al-Ghariani zawiya has been extensively restored and it is now the headquarters of the Association for the safeguard of the Medina of Kairouan and the regional branch of the National Institute of Archaeology and Art.

47 - Decoration of the external mihrab.

44

MASGID B. KHAYRUN OR THE MOSQUE OF THE THREE DOORS

Kairouan is known as the city «of three hundred mosques». In spite of successive renovations and the disappearance of certain mosques, the medina of Kairouan still counts a large number of ancient small neighbourhood mosques, most of which are still in-situ and bear the names of their original founders : Masgid 'Abdallah, masgid al-Ansar, masgid Abi-Maysara, masgid al-Hubuli etc...

In addition to these small mosques, since the XVIIIth and XIXth century, a considerable number of Zawiyas and mausoleums have been built by the people of Kairouan to commemorate illustrious citizens. All these religious buildings have undoubtedly made Kairouan the spiritual capital of the country.

Amongst these masgids or small mosques, the Ibn Khayrun mosque, known as the mosque of the Three Doors is one of the rare buildings to have preserved its architectural aspect and especially its elaborately decorated IXth century facade.

Situated in the heart of the medina, in one of the oldest quarters of Kairouan, this mosque was built in 252H (AD866) by Mohammed b. Khayrun al Ma'afiri, originally from Andalousia. Despite the alterations it underwent, notably the addition of a minaret in 844H (AD1440) it has retained its very fine carved stone facade dating from the Aghlabid period.

This facade constitutes the focal point of the building. Three doors lead directly into the prayer hall. The doors are crowned by three horseshoe arches. The decoration of the facade is made up of several registers running the whole width of the building.

The decoration is bordered on the top and bottom by a series of sculptured stone corbels.

48 - *External facade of the Masgid b. Khayrun or the Mosque of the Three Doors.*

Three bands of inscriptions mention the date of the building, the name of its founder and the third, written in corser script, indicates the date when the mosque was restored and the minaret added.

The middle register is decorated with floral motifs composed of demi-palmettes, three-lobed or polylobed leaves interspaced with medallions ornamented with eight-lobed leaves.

The facade of the mosque of the Three Doors is an example of the wealth of the Aghlabid architectural and ornamental repertory. The IXth century Kairouan school inspired and served as a model for buildings built all over the western basin of Islam for several centuries.

49 - *Decorative elements adorning the facade of the mosque.*

SIDI AMOR ABADA MUSEUM

50 - External view of the vast architectural complex of Sidi Amor Abada, XIXth century.

This museum was established in a Zawiya built in 1872 and it contains Sidi Amor Abada's tomb : it is a huge architectural ensemble characterized by its seven cupolas. The cupolas are similar to the type seen in Kairouan over the last ten centuries or more.

The Zawiya is the work of an outstanding figure who marked Kairouan life during the first half of the XIXth century. His name was Amor b. Salem b. Sa'ad b. Miftah al 'Ayari from the Ouled Ayar tribe. He was known under the name of Sidi Amor Abada and he was a blacksmith.

He was quite a remarkable personage, enigmatic and with an astounding force of character and great faith, exceedingly powerful and grand.

Amar Abada was very popular in the region and especially in rural areas. The people of Kairouan venerated him and at the same time feared him, probably because he was on good terms with the central power of the beys : Mustapha and Ahmed Bey.

Oral tradition has woven tales and myths around this figure which to this day are retained in our collective memory.

A large room of the Zawiya has been transformed into a museum displaying objects that belonged to Sidi Amor Abada or were made by him. These objects are quite useless in view of their gigantic size and must certainly be an indication of their creator's megalomania : Giant anchors, designed, it is said, to protect Kairouan by maintaining it soldered to the country, heavy swords, a colossal pipe, very heavy bronze pestles, weapon-holders, trunks, doors, standards, etc...

All these pieces date from the middle of the XIXth century and they all bear carved inscriptions. The text of these inscriptions is in fact the story of Sidi Amor Abada's life, his origins, his family, his conception of life, his relations with society, with authority...

51 - Sidi Amar Abada's cenotaph.

52 - Rack for holding arms adorned with engraved inscriptions.

53 - One of Sidi 'Amor 'Abada's many very heavy swords.

48

BI'R RUTA OR BARRUTA WELL

54 - Barruta Well, room with the well.

This well is considered to be the oldest in Kairouan. Not much is known of its history. The name Bi'r Ruta deformed into Barruta is only mentioned for the first time in the Vth century H or XIth century AD. Certain written sources referring to the history of Kairouan attribute it to the Abbasid governor Harthama in the year 180 H or AD796.

The fact that the history of this well remains unclear, has meant that collective memory has created and transmitted legends on the subject and popular religious belief has surrounded it with veneration. It is believed that the water of the well communicates with the water of Bi'r Zem-Zem, the famous sacred well of Mecca. Another legend claims that he who tastes of the Barruta water will surely return to Kairouan one day.

The present building housing the well dates from the Muradite period. An inscription attributes its restoration to Mohammed Bey b. Murad in 1100H (AD1690). A number of annexes were built around the well including the room that houses the well itself, where a cammel works a noria to raise water.

This room is covered by an arched cupola inspired from the first IXth century Kairouan cupolas. There are also a few dwellings and a prayer hall on the outside wall of which stands a fountain with a drinking trough.

55 - External view of the well, one of the oldest of Kairouan.

THE RAQQADA NATIONAL MUSEUM
OF ISLAMIC ART

Housed in a splendid former presidential palace, this museum contains precious and rare homogenous collections from archaeological sites around Kairouan, notably Raqqada and Sabra al-Mansouriyya as well as objets having belonged to the monuments of the city, mainly the great mosque.

Situated at Raqqada in the Kairouan country side, 10 km south west of the city on the Sfax road, it is an important archaeological site, as Raqqada was the second royal town of the Agh-labid emirs. The museum covers a surface area of more than 20 hectars and it is built in the middle of vast grounds surrounded by a wall.

The entrance hall contains a superb wooden model on a 1/50 scale of the great mosque of Kairouan with a cut on the level of the minaret and the central nave showing the detail of the structures of the building. This model enables visitors to take in this huge ensemble and appreciate the harmony of its plan.

Opposite this model, a copy of the mosque's mihrab sculpted in stucco is displayed. It is composed of twenty-eight pannels arranged in seven vertical registers of four elements. The pannels, with an openwork or champleve decoration, are ornamented with floral and geometrical motifs.

56 - Entrance to the museum.

A chronological table of the different dynasties that ruled over Ifriqiya since the Arab conquest in AD 648 to the end of the Muradite dynasty at the beginning of the XVIIIth century enables visitors to situate the different chronological stages of the history of the country.

CERAMICS ROOM

This room offers an important collection of ceramics from the Aghlabid IXth century and the Fatimid Xth century, essentially taken from the sites of Raqqada and Sabra.

The Aghlabid exhibits are characterized by the use of three dominant colours : olive green, brown to outline it and the yellow constitutes the background. They present three types of decoration : an essentially epigraphic ornament, the central motif being composed of the repetition of the one word al-Mulk (sovereignty). The second type combines a large variety of floral and geometric motifs and is indicative of a rich and creative imagination. The third type portrays animal forms, essentially birds, represented in a static and stylized form.

57 - Raqqada. Aghlabid ceramic bowl decorated with birds and chequered design. IIIrd century H. (IXth century AD).

58 - Raqqada. Aghlabid plate decorated with floral and geometric motifs. IIIrd century H. (IXth century AD).

There are two clearly distinguishable groups of Fatimid ceramics : the first is considered to be locally produced, and comes from the site of Sabra. The ceramics have metallic glints and portray animated figures as a central motif : birds, hares, antilopes, most often stylized, or human figures : a prince with a long tunic holding a chalice in his hand, a person on horseback... The second group comes from Egypt and is also glazed and is characterized by a preference for animal figures with fabulous or mythological aspects.

Of particular interest is a beautiful plate found at Sabra but considered to be imported. It is decorated with a hunting scene with falcons and its Irno-Mesopotamian influence is quite apparent.

59 - Sabra Al Mansouriya. Fatimid plate with the figure of a prince holding a cup with two scrolls. IVth century H. (Xth century AD).

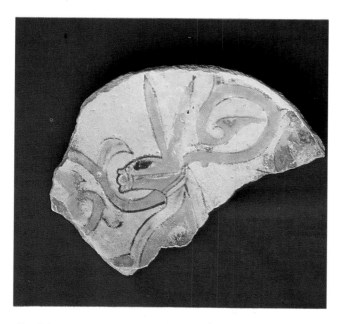

60 - *Sabra Al Mansouriya. Fragment of a Fatimid plate decorated with a rabbit represented in a stylized form. IVth century H (Xth century AD).*

THE COIN ROOM

This room contains a very important coin collection that traces the economic history of Ifriqiya over a period of more than six centuries. The inscriptions on the coins provide information on certain aspects of economic life and constitute a convincing barometer of the economy : quality of the metal employed, weight, date and place of minting, the formula employed and the way in which it evolved, etc..

The coins are essentially dinars and dirhems. The gold coins, the dinars, weigh 4.25 g while the silver coins weigh only 7/10ths, 2,9 g according to the table of measures adopted by the Umayyad caliph Abd al-Malik ibn Marwan.

One of the schowcases is devoted to the different mints of the Umayyad and Abbasid periods. There were mints all over the Islamic world : Ifriqiya, Andalousia, Egypt, Wasit, Nishpur, Basra, Tashkent.

Despite the variety of horizons it is apparent that the dirhem are of the same shape, carry the same formula and have similar stamps thereby illustrating the political and economic unity of the Moslem world during the first centuries of the hegira.

A map of Tunisia indicates where the ancient mints in Ifriqiya were located. Although one notes the names of certain cities such as Tunis, Sfax, Mahdiya, Tozer, it is obvious that the mints were mainly concentrated around Kairouan, al-Abbasiya, Sabra al-Mansouriyya and the city of «the glory of Islam».

The remainder of the collection is displayed in chronological order by dynasty; Aghlabid money which was much sought after in the western Mediterranean, Fatimid money characterized by the Shiite formula, was of sterling quality; the Zirid period, the Almohado-Hafsid and the Ottoman money.

A very rare piece of money was coined during the Fatimid period : the Kharigite Abu Yazid, known as the man on a donkey, dinar. The latter rose against the Fatimids, took Kairouan and forced al-Qaim to take refuge at Mahdiya. Abu Yazid struck his own coins in the year 333H (AD944).

61 - Aghlabid dinar.

62 - Fatimid dinar.

THE ROOM WITH THE CUPOLA

It is the most beautiful room of the museum and its superb cupola, its elaborate decoration, its stained glass windows and its view on the park attract the attention of visitors.

The room contains precious glass, lead and bronze objects.

Glassware : the majority of these pieces were found on the site of Sabra al-Mansouriyya : decanters, tumblers, perfume flasks, blown glass sprinklers, lamps. They are either moulded or blown and decorated with engraved motifs or adorned with applications of glass threads. The many fragments of flasks, handles, necks and bases are most often white but may also be peacock blue or jade green. These objects are indicative of the degree of development of the manufacture of glass in Ifriqiya. Historical textes mention the existence in Kairouan, at the end of the VIIIth century, of a quarter or a souk entirely devoted to glasswork. Recent excavations on the site of Raqqada and especially Sabra and Mahdiya have brought to light several kilns.

Other pieces made of glass, dating from the first centuries of the hegira consist of coins used as standards for money. These stamps in the form of glass disks and bearing an epigraphic print in relief served both as a guarantee and as a means of grading in measuring capacity.

Lead : an important collection of lead weights discovered at Raqqada date from the Aghlabid and Fatimid eras. Each weight bears the seal of the governor or the prince, guaranteeing the authenticity of the weights.

63 - Museum's room with a cupola.

64 - Sabra Al Mansouriya. Glass decanter, flask and water sprinkler. Fatimid era IVth century H (Xth century AD).

65 - Sabra Al Mansouriya. Glass decanter. VIth century H (Xth century AD).

Bronze chandeliers : These consist of bronze chandeliers from the great mosque in Kairouan. They are attached to the ceiling by three chains. They look like circular trays with the edges and the centre dotted with circular slots to lodge glass globes. Their decoration is varied, either floral or geometric, with three-lobed or heart-shaped leaves, stylized vine leaves, equidistant arches, circular rings, crosses... These chandeliers date from the XIth century.

But one of the finest pieces of the museum is without a doubt the famous lantern of the Zirid emir, al-Muizz b. Badis that lit his maq-sura in the great mosque.

It is a large openwork copper lantern composed of a central belly and three narrow plates attached to a small cupola equipped with a suspension hook. The decoration of this lantern is achieved by perforation. It is constituted essentially of geometric and epigraphic designs. One of the three texts mentions the name of the brass-founder who made the lantern and that of the sovereign al-Muizz to whom it seems to have been destined «... the work of Mohammed b. Ali al-Qaysi as-Saffar for al-Muizz...» Vth century of the hegira (XIth century AD).

66 - Al Mu'izz b. Badis Lantern, Vth century H. (XIth century AD).

67 - Detail of the lantern.

KORAN ROOM

This room contains very fine pages of the Koran on parchment. These Kairouan parchments, by their number and quality, constitute one of the finest and rarest collections of the Islamic world. Originally, they were part of a large collection of manuscripts kept in the old library of the great mosque of Kairouan to which they were bequeathed and constituted into a habous. (Similar to a trust fund).

A showcase is devoted to the famous Koran on blue parchment written in elegant kufic calligraphy all in gold lettering. Several other fine Korans can be admired, bequeathed to the great mosque by the Zirid ruler and other members of his family, such as the al-Muizz b. Badis Koran and the Koran of Fatima al-Hadina, Badis' governess, which dates from 410H (AD 1020) and the Korans of the princesses Um-Malal and Um-al-Ulu respectively al-Muizz's grandmother and sister.

In some cases, the inside cover pages of the Korans provide precious information on the preparation of the parchment and the leather, on the calligraphy and the binding and on the illuminations as well as mentioning the date of the koran or at least the date on which it was constituted a habous.

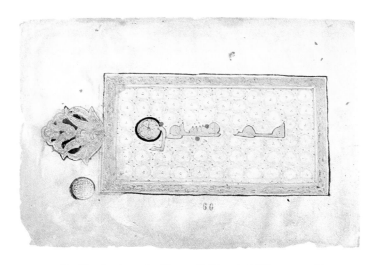

68 - Illumination of a Koran, Zirid period Vth century H.

69 - Page of a Koran on parchment.

70 - Koran on blue parchment. Vth century H. (Xth century AD).

The inside cover of Fatima's Koran indicates that it was Ali b. Ahmed al-Warraq who wrote, vowelled, gilded and bound the Koran in 410H...

The manuscripts are adorned with rich gold illuminations. Fine floral and vegetal motifs cover a surface outlined or interspersed with interlacing.

The ink used for these Korans was of a rich brown or black for the letters, red and blue for the vowels. Al-Muizz's Koran is particular in that small red green and yellow dots are used.

The ink was obtained from gall nut and gum-arabic. A IIIrd century H (IXth century AD) Koran uses safran to retrace the decoration and egg white as a fixative. Finally, a great many Korans were written entirely in gold letter.

Through the diversity of their form, the elegance of their calligraphy and their elaborate decoration, these parchment Korans are a further illustration of the degree of evolution and the prosperity of the art of manuscript and parchment in Kairouan.

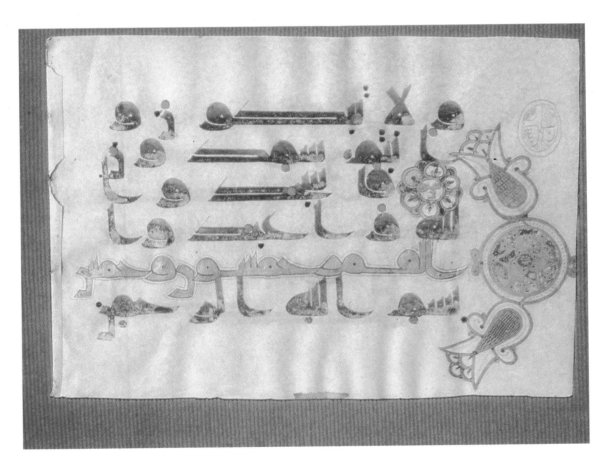

71 - Koran on parchment with fine kufic writing.

In addition to visiting the museum itself, a visit should be made to the museum's laboratories, notably the laboratory for the restoration and safeguarding of manuscripts and parchment, where the latest techniques in restoration can be observed, as well as to the ceramics laboratory and the photo and microfilm laboratory.

An extension to the museum is shortly to be opened and this will make room for large collections hitherto unknown to the public such as the ancient painted wooden beams from the ceilings of the great mosque, dating from IXth to XIth centuries AD, with their sumptuous decoration, as well as a stone garden where funerary stelae from Kairouan with their remarkable paleographic and ornamental richness will be displayed for the public to admire.

72 - Kairouan tombstone with engraved writing. 256 H. Aghlabid period.

73 - Stele in the form of a column, Zirid period.

74 - Quadrangular stele adorned with an arch shaped design. End of the Zirid period.

Contents

Photographic credits

Ridha Zili : 7 - 9 - 20 - 15 - 23 - 28 - 29 - 33 - 42 - 50 - 54 - 57 - 58 - 64 - 65 - 66 - 69 - 70 - 71.

Abdelaziz Frikha : 3 - 18 - 19 - 20 - 35 - 36 - 55 - 63.

Jacques Perez : 49.

Abderrazak Khechine : 1 - 2 - 4 - 6 - 11 - 12 - 13 - 14 - 16 - 17 - 21 - 22 - 24 - 25 - 26 - 27 - 30 - 31 - 32 - 34 - 37 - 39 - 40 - 41 - 43 - 44
45 - 46 - 47 - 48 - 51 - 52 - 59 - 60 - 61 - 62 - 67 - 68 - 72 - 73 - 74.

Goodman : 38.

Raqqada Museum : 53 - 56.

*The National Heritage Agency wishes to thank the O.N.T.T.
for its cooperation with the iconographic documentation.*

Imprimerie Tunis Carthage
Septembre - 1992